Rooms of the Living

Cover Art: www.123rf.com

Author Photo: Paul Martin
Cover and text design by Katherine Wintersteen
Titles and text set in Birch and Justus

Printed on acid-free paper.

Coal Hill Review is an imprint of Autumn House Press, a nonprofit corporation with the mission of publishing and promoting poetry and other fine literature.

Coal Hill Review Staff
Editor-in-Chief: Michael Simms
Managing Editor: Caroline Tanski
Assistant Editors: Giuliana Certo, Christine Stroud

PENNSYLVANIA COUNCIL ON THE ARTS

Autumn House Press receives state arts funding support through a grant from the Pennsylvania Council on the Arts, a state agency funded by the Commonwealth of Pennsylvania, and the National Endowment for the Arts, a federal agency.

ISBN: 978-1-932870-84-8 + 90000

Rooms of the Living

poems by
Paul Martin

Coal Hill Review • Pittsburgh, Pennsylvania

Contents

For my family, the seen and the unseen

The Regulator

Its long, brown wooden case hung
on the kitchen wall in the first house,
the heavy, brass pendulum moving
deliberately above my grandmother standing
over the coal stove stuffing pork with garlic
and baking trays of halupkies,
moving above the three generations
elbow to elbow around the table,
above the evening penny card games,
above my mother at the window, dishes washed,
watching the sun set over the zinc plant,
above my grandfather reading his Slovak bible
as everyone else went up to bed.
It stood above the busy lives deaf
to its sound and above the boy, alone
in the house, dust motes rising through slanted light,
the clock clicking him into loss.

The Miracle of Television

My grandmother told my brother and me
rolling around the floor
in front of the snowy black and white screen
to sit up straight and behave
because they could see us, and she wasn't joking
or trying to fool two kids buzzed on tall Pepsis
into the quiet she deserved
after another day over the stove
and the steaming tubs of clothes in the basement,
a sweet, generous soul from the old country
who spoke broken English.
She really believed it, not so big a leap, really, as the one
she took when she left Czechoslovakia for the land
of promised work, grinding as it was,
and two kinds of roasts for Sunday dinner
and now a machine that somehow
brought people from distant cities through the wires
into her front room on Lehigh Street
where Eddie Cantor rolled his wide eyes
and soft shoed his way into her heart,
and where Jimmy Durante put on his topcoat and hat,
and started singing "Good Night," turning and walking away
through smaller and smaller spotlights, stopping
to look back at the short, round woman in a flowered apron
sitting in her stuffed chair, perfectly attentive,
her worn hands folded carefully on her lap.

My Mother the Dancer

Louis Prima, Fats Domino, Rosemary Clooney, she piled
high the 45's, grabbed the mop she called her *honey*
and began upstairs, singing and swinging it

across the floor, dipping low to reach under the beds,
shaking it out the window, sweeping
her dust cloth across the dressers, picking

up a stray sock, or underwear, circling
through the three bedrooms and down
the stairs, moving as though a curtain had opened

to one of those Hollywood musicals
she dragged us to at the Rialto, pulling me by the arm
out of the chair I was sunken into, twirling me

once or twice around her, that red bandanna
in her black hair as she danced toward my brother,
urging him into the sunlight slanting through the window.

Cucumbers

Still days away from the first ripe tomato,
I pick another dozen cucumbers
to give to the neighbors and see my mother
slicing them into a bowl, each layer
sprinkled with salt, then setting them aside
for awhile before squeezing out the bitterness,
adding vinegar and sour cream
to just the right balance.

When my father comes home from his work
with crowbar and spike hammer
on the railroad section gang,
she'll set before him the cold bowlful,
a buttered hunk of rye bread
and, until he's finished, some quiet.

Fitting

In front of the salesman my mother
is speaking to me in Slovak,

saying the coat I like isn't warm
enough, saying, *ye to prilis tesne**

even as I'm shrinking
inside it, with each word from her mouth

praying she'll stop
so the whole store will quit staring

and we can both disappear
into English.

*it's much too tight

First Frost

We stared out the kitchen
windows at the white lawn.

In the garden the sweet basil
I intended to turn into pesto

had turned dark. Tomatoes slumped
over their tall cages, shrunken,

their green reaching done.
By the time I walked into the sharp air

the frost, under the advancing sun,
had withdrawn,

except for that spot under the mulberry tree
that became, on a closer look,

the mockingbird's ash-gray feathers
left behind by a hawk.

Blood Prayer

*Vyslobods nas, Pan,** I whisper
to myself as the ambulance screams
past the house, Slovak words
my grandfather spoke
whenever a siren or a funeral
lifted his head from his soup
or the ground he was planting,
words that rise in me now,
sitting in darkness,
watching the passed houses glow
for a moment in red.

*deliver us, Lord

Mock Orange

(For Lonnie, in Memoriam)

Buried in a shoe box of fading photographs is one
of you, a sun-browned boy
wearing a red, white and blue T-shirt
circled with the words *swim-surf-sun-run*,
standing under the bowed branches
of the mock orange, staring warily
into the camera, idling for a moment
before you race away to play with your brother

in the yard where I sit twenty years later
watching the sun burn down
behind the hill, the air suddenly heavy
with the sweetness of mock orange.
Looking over my shoulder I find the space
where you stood, the white blossoms
growing luminous in the dusk.
Barely arrived to full bloom, they drop,
one, then two and three together,
onto the darkening lawn.

Tourists

The restaurant deck overlooking the lower Niagara
is closed, tables and chairs taken inside
for the winter. The only one here, I stare
down at the wide, green river,
the swirling gulls, a fisherman's small outboard.
If you were with me, I'd tell you what I learned
from the book I was reading this morning:
that 11,000 years ago the Falls stood here
in Lewiston, its crest eroding
the seven miles south to where they are now;
that in 50,000 more years, they'll retreat,
foot by foot, twenty miles to Lake Erie
and cease to exist, numbers that might move us
to silence or my joking *I'll be an old man by then*,
this cold, wind-blasted gorge driving us
to a cozy pub where we'd settle in with the locals,
asking, as we usually do, about where to find
the best Italian, or a good beef on 'weck.
We'd reminisce about favorite haunts long closed,
and the city we loved, now in ruins—
in the drinks and small talk feeling the warmth
of one brief tourist for another.

The Coming Thaw

The canal ice is littered
with stones boys have thrown
trying to break through the thickness.
When the thaw comes, the sudden warmth
will call the boys out in T-shirts
to play ball or turn their heads
for the first time toward a passing girl,
and the frozen-tight world will unfasten,
the forgotten stones dropping,
first the heaviest,
splashless toward the bottom.

The June Garden

Barefoot in the wet grass, I stare
at the scarred cherry tree
I almost put the chainsaw to, now in full leaf,
and the brick patio I laid down
with its café table, four chairs
and an unobstructed view of the sky.
How lucky I am the light finds me
here on this curve on Levans Road
where the sticky buds
of the peonies come unglued
to creamy white, and swallows glide
into the birdhouse swaying
on a pole above tomatoes and peppers.
How merciful that the mind forgets
for a while the pain
on the other side of the hedges,
intrigued as it is by the Brown Thrasher's swiping
aside last year's decaying leaves
to find underneath the fat grub.

Morning at the Lake

The last one to wake, I hear
voices, soft laughter
rising from the kitchen,

the aroma of coffee and toast.
After last night's thunderstorm
the air so light and clear.

Oh, how glad I am
to slowly take on flesh
and enter the rooms of the living.

Small Town Sunday Pastoral

Except for the gray pensioner with the cane
staring into Shea's closed hardware store,
Delaware Avenue's deserted,
a shimmering quiet over the town.
Through a window open on Lehigh Street
the murmur of a baseball game.
A bachelor who spent a late night
at the Sokol Hall dozes on a front room couch.
In the shade of a back yard grape arbor
a woman still in her apron settles into the paper.
Her husband in the sleeveless T-shirt waters
his tall, purple delphiniums,
while a yellow dog strays down the dirt alley
where a boy bounces a rubber ball
off a peeling shed back to himself.
Someone is drawn back to a kitchen
to pick at the leftover roast.
From Hazard Road to Residence Park
it's slow and easy: the usual
weekday arguments exhausted,
the only siren Helen Babarsky on a chaise lounge
sunning herself in red halter and shorts,
and the one who's slipping away
comes back through the screen door
with two quarts of ice cream,
one butter pecan and one cherry vanilla,
just as those who love him
notice he's gone.

Love Poem Ending with
a Phrase from Stern

Waiting on the porch for my wife
to join me for a movie and dinner,

I wonder about the life
I might have lived if I hadn't stopped

into the candy store I was passing
that night forty-five years ago

and continued down Falls Street
into some different life my imagination is trying

hard to follow through the maze of streets
and years when Rita steps out the door

smiling and walks beside me to the car,
goosing me, earthy as she is, into a laugh,

into the closeness of hands and eyes,
into my one, lucky life.

Turning Back the Clock

Because it tasted so good last night
tonight I cooked it again: *linguine
alla puttanesca*, spicy with hot peppers,

garlic, anchovies and black olives
and again we ate too much,
sopping up the sauce with crusty bread,

drinking the same dark wine,
listening again to Billie Holiday sing
"It Had to Be You" and "Sleepy Time

Down South." Again we lingered
over cleaned plates, talking about nothing important
enough to remember the next morning,

then lay together on the couch, unbuttoning
each other, the only sound the clock
I turned back on our way upstairs.

Acknowledgements

Thanks to the editors of *Christian Science Monitor* where "My Mother the Dancer" was first published, and to the *Southern Poetry Review* where "Tourists" originally appeared.

Thanks to Rita and Elizabeth for their unfailing love and their faith in the poems.

Thanks to my friends, Harry Humes, Steve Myers, and Jim Murphy, for their insightful and constructive suggestions that improved the poems.

Thanks to my brothers, Mike, Fritz, and John, for helping me to remember.

Paul Martin's poems have appeared in *America, Atlanta Review, Big Muddy, Boulevard, The Christian Science Monitor, Commonweal, 5 AM, Green Mountains Review, New Letters, Nimrod, Poetry East, Poet Lore, Prairie Schooner, River Styx, Southern Humanities Review, Southern Poetry Review, Tar River, Texas Poetry Review, Yankee* and other journals. His book, *Closing Distances*, twice a finalist in the National Poetry Series, was published in 2009 by *The Backwaters Press*. Martin is the author of three chapbooks: *Green Tomatoes, Walking Away Waving*, and *Morning on Canal Street*, and has been awarded two poetry fellowships from the Pennsylvania Council on the Arts. He lives in Ironton, PA with his wife, Rita.

The Coal Hill Review Chapbook Series

**Co-winner of the 2012
Coal Hill Chapbook Prize**
Rooms of the Living
Paul Martin

**Co-winner of the 2012
Coal Hill Chapbook Prize**
Prayers of an American Wife
Victoria Kelly

A Coal Hill Special Edition
Irish Coffee
Jay Carson

**Winner of the 2011
Coal Hill Chapbook Prize**
Bathhouse Betty
Matt Terhune

A Coal Hill Special Edition
Crossing Laurel Run
Maxwell King

**Winner of the 2010
Coal Hill Chapbook Prize**
Shelter
Gigi Marks

**Winner of the 2009
Coal Hill Chapbook Prize**
Shake It and It Snows
Gailmarie Pahmeier

**Winner of the 2008
Coal Hill Chapbook Prize**
The Ghetto Exorcist
James Tyner